This edition
© Robert Frederick Ltd.
Montague House, Lambridge St,
Bath BA1 6RX

First published 1996

Printed in Singapore

Dobby's 75th

THE LITTLE BOOK OF HANDY HINTS

ANIMAL HAIR

Use sellotape to remove animal
hair from clothes, furniture etc.
Simply wrap the sellotape around
your fingers (sticky side outward)
and rub over the hairs.

ANTS

Discourage ants in the house by
sprinkling bicarbonate of soda
or powdered borax of cloves on
shelves and in drawers.

ASH

Do not empty these into a wastepaper basket as they can easily start a fire. A large tin is much more suitable.

To prevent cigarette ends from burning in an ashtray and to reduce the smell of stale tobacco, coat the bottom of the ashtray with baking powder.

BAKING TINS

To discourage a new baking tin
from rusting, rub inside and out
with lard and place in an oven
at moderate heat for 45 minutes.
When cool wipe thoroughly
with a paper towel.

To remove rust from tinware rub
with half a raw potato that has
been dipped in scouring powder.
Rinse and dry in an oven.

BALL POINT PENS

If a ballpoint pen doesn't work
try warming the point gently
with a match or by pouring
boiling water over it.

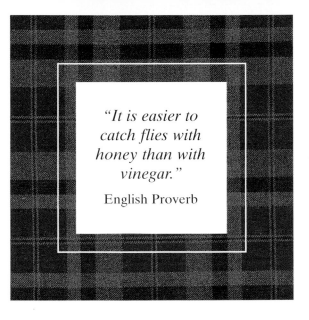

> *"It is easier to catch flies with honey than with vinegar."*
>
> English Proverb

BARBECUE

To maximise the heat, line your barbecue with tin-foil, shiny side up. Use left over brewed coffee to clean the barbecue set.

BATHS

If you have unsightly stains on your bath or wash basin due to a dripping tap, try rubbing with a paste made of lemon juice and salt and rinsing well.

Failing this, try rubbing them with a toothbrush using a paste of cream of tartar and peroxide and then rinsing.

BOOKS

To keep your books in good condition do not place them tight against a wall, but leave a couple of centimetres gap to enable the air to circulate around them. Also, make sure they are kept upright and not leaning at an angle as this would be bad for their bindings.

BOTTLES

Stick an adhesive plaster over the cork of the bottle containing liquid when packing to help prevent accidents.

Remove strong odours from bottles by filling them with a mixture of cold water and four teaspoons of dry mustard and then leaving them to stand for a least half a day before rinsing well.

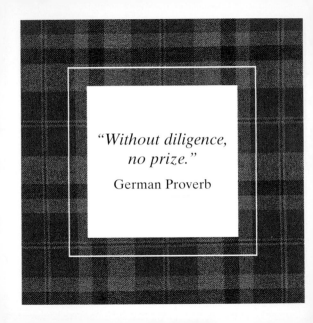

*"Without diligence,
no prize."*

German Proverb

BREAD BOARDS

If your wooden bread board is warped, place the board on a flat surface and cover it with a wet cloth, leaving it for at least 24 hours.

BROOMS

When a broom handle
does not fit anymore then wrap
with adhesive tape and screw
the handle back into the socket.
This should help keep it
in place.

CANDLES

To increase the life span of candles store in the freezer for a few hours before use.

To make candles fit into candle sticks dip the end in hot water until it is soft enough to fit into the required size.

CAR

To prevent bumping your car in a tight garage attach an old tyre to the wall.

To clean a very dirty car use a mixture of methylated spirit and water (1 unit of methylated spirit to 8 units of water). Do not rinse. This should leave your car shining.

CARPETS

To restore the life to carpet pile which has been flattened by furniture legs, place several layers of wet cloth onto the area. Then hold a hot iron lightly on top of the cloth. The steam should bring back the bounce to the carpet which you should then be able to fluff up using a nail brush.

CHINA

Protect your best china plates
from chips and cracks by
alternating them with paper
plates or corrugated paper
when storing them or when
packing them.

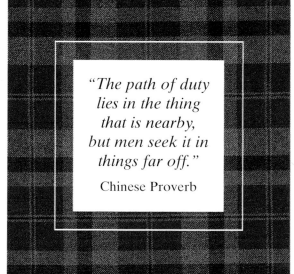

"*The path of duty
lies in the thing
that is nearby,
but men seek it in
things far off.*"

Chinese Proverb

COOKING SMELLS

Get rid of unwanted cooking smells by boiling one teaspoon of ground cinnamon or ground cloves in a $\frac{1}{4}$ litre of water for fifteen minutes.

CORK

Cork expands. If it does not
fit back into the bottle then
place it in boiling water for a
few minutes until it becomes
soft. It will then fit easily
back into the bottle.

CRYSTAL

To give a real sparkle to your crystal add a few drops of ammonia to the washing water and vinegar to the rinsing water.

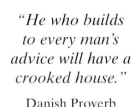

*"He who builds
to every man's
advice will have a
crooked house."*

Danish Proverb

DECORATING

When you have decorated a room, make sure you keep a note of the number of rolls of wallpaper or tins of paint that you used, so that when you come to redecorating, you will know exactly what you need.

DISHWASHERS

Pour 4 heaped tablespoons
of bicarbonate of soda
through the bottom rack of
your dishwasher and put it
on the rinse cycle to
refresh the smell.

DRAWERS

If you have trouble opening
tight fitting drawers, rub soap or
candle wax along the upper
edges to lubricate them.

DRILLING

To stop the drill from slipping when drilling a hole into metal or ceramic tiles, cover the mark with adhesive tape, drill through it and then remove the tape.

When drilling into the ceiling, drill through the base of a transparent plastic container to catch the chips and protect your eyes.

ELECTRIC-WIRE

When fitting a plug it is often
difficult to cut the rubber which
encompasses the wire without
cutting the copper thread. If you
warm the rubber with a match
you will be able to strip it very
easily with your fingers.

ENAMEL

If your enamel is cracked and the cracks become dirty, make a thick paste of French chalk and water and coat the enamel with it. Leave it until the paste dries out and begins to crack and then brush off. Repeat until the cracks come clean.

FELT-TIPPED PENS

If your felt-tip pen seems to have run out, try dipping the tip in a little vinegar – this should give it a new lease of life.

Store felt-tip pens tip downwards with the cap on so that they are always ready to use.

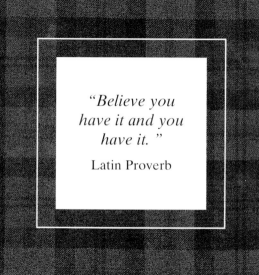

"*Believe you
have it and you
have it.*"

Latin Proverb

FINGER NAILS

Never cut nails with scissors as
this can cause them to split.
File them with an emery board
– from the sides up to the tip
(and never in a see-saw
movement) – as this is softer
than a metal file.

FIREPLACES

If lighting a fire in a chimney
which has not been used for some
time and which may be damp,
first burn a creased sheet of
newspaper in the grate to remove
moisture from the chimney.

Don't burn coloured magazines
or newspaper as coloured ink gives
off lead vapour when burning.

FLIES

A pleasant way of discouraging flies is to place cotton wool balls sprinkled with a few drops of lavender oil on saucers around the room. Basil or mint grown in pots on the windowsill or in a window box is also a sweet smelling deterrent.

FLOORS

Talcum powder sprinkled
between floorboards will help
to prevent squeaking.

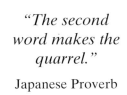

"The second word makes the quarrel."

Japanese Proverb

FLOWERS

If picking flowers from the garden, do not do it during the warmest part of the day as the flowers will not last long. Pick them in the early morning or early evening if you want them to last longer.

FRAMING

Insert kitchen foil behind the picture when framing to prevent damage from damp.

FREEZER

After defrosting your freezer
try rubbing the inside with
glycerine. Next time you come
to defrost it you should find that
the ice will come away easily.

To stop packages from sticking to
the freezer sides, do not put them
straight back into the freezer after
defrosting but leave the freezer
empty for half an hour first.

FURNITURE

When it is exposed to direct sunlight, polished furniture will permanently lose its veneer. To avoid lasting damage, either position the piece of furniture elsewhere, or keep it covered with a cloth.

FUSES

Keep a torch and a card of
fuse wire beside the fuse box in
case of an emergency.

GARDEN TOOLS

To remove ruse from your garden tools use wire wool dipped in turpentine.

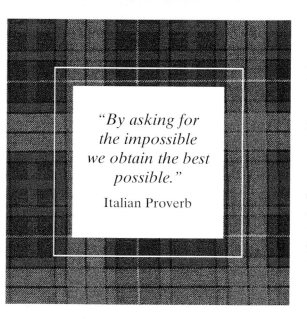

"*By asking for the impossible we obtain the best possible.*"

Italian Proverb

GARLIC

To remove the smell of garlic from your breath try chewing some fresh mint, a coffee bean, a stalk of parsley or celery or some cardamom seeds!

GIFT WRAP

When you are wrapping large numbers of presents, at Christmas for example or at a children's party, try using attractive leftover wallpaper which makes a far cheaper alternative to gift wrap.

GLASSES

If two glasses stick together, stand the bottom glass in hot (not boiling) water and fill the top one with cold water. This should cause them to separate without damaging them.

Stand a silver spoon in a glass or jar to prevent it from cracking when boiling water is poured into it.

GLUE

Fit a piece of candle on the top
of a glue bottle and use it as a
stopper to close the bottle.
As glue does not stick to candle
wax you should no longer
have any problems when you
come to open it.

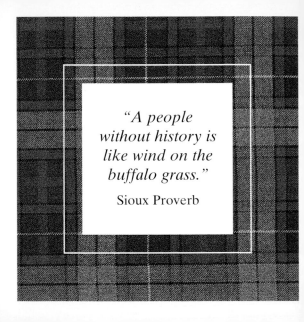

"A people without history is like wind on the buffalo grass."

Sioux Proverb

GRASS

To prevent grass from growing
between the cracks in your
paving stones or path, sprinkle
salt in them, or pour on very
salted boiling water.

GREENFLY

Help to discourage greenfly by
planting garlic around the plants
that attract the greenfly.
When the garlic starts sprouting,
keep the shoots cut back.

GUTTERS

A piece of chicken wire
placed over the top of your
gutter will effectively
prevent falling leaves from
blocking it.

HARD WATER DEPOSITS

If you find hard water deposits in jugs or vases etc., fill with malt vinegar and leave for a few hours. Rub off with a fine wire scouring pad and rinse thoroughly.

HOSE

To make the hose fit easily onto the tap rub the inside of the hose with some soap. The soap will quickly dry when the hose is fitted.

HOT-WATER BOTTLES

When filling a hot-water bottle you should lie it flat on its back holding the neck upright. This will prevent the water splashing due to air-bubbles in the bottle.

Add a little salt to the water to keep it warm longer.

*"Good luck
comes to the
saucy and bold."*

Welsh Proverb

INSECTS

By hanging a fresh bunch of stinging nettles in front of any open windows or doors, you can discourage flies and wasps from invading your house.

IRONING

Starch can be removed from the bottom of your iron by sprinkling some fine kitchen salt onto a piece of paper and rubbing the iron over it until the base becomes smooth again, or by rubbing the base with half a lemon dipped in fine kitchen salt.

IVORY

If you would like to keep small pieces of ivory white, place them in the direct sunlight.

Very dirty ivory can be cleaned by leaving the item to soak for a few hours in milk and then washing it with warm soapy water.

JARS

Put a few drops of bleach in a glass jar to remove strong fish or pickle smells. Leave for at least twelve hours.

Make some small holes in the lid of a glass screw-topped jar with a nail or skewer, to use it as a cheap flour dredger or water sprinkler when ironing.

*"Luck is one half
of success."*

Hindu Proverb

JAR LABELS

Do not label your jars until the
contents have cooled, otherwise
the labels will come unstuck.

JEWELLERY

To give a quick shine to gold jewellery, rub with a ball of soft bread. For silver jewellery to shine, rub with half a lemon and then rinse off before drying.

To loosen or remove a ring from your finger, wash your hands with soap and water and try to take the ring off while the soap is still on your hands.

KETTLES

Place a marble in your kettle to prevent it from furring.

Alternatively, pour in a small quantity of vinegar (enough to cover the element where applicable), bring it to the boil then agitate it. Leave it to cool and then rinse thoroughly. It may be necessary to repeat these processes several times.

KEYS

Covering a rusty key with turpentine and leaving it to soak for a couple of hours before rubbing and drying it should bring its shine back.

KNITWEAR

To prevent your knitwear
from stretching when you
are washing it in the
washing machine, place it
first inside a pillowcase.

LEATHER SHOES

When drying leather shoes or boots, never be tempted to do so quickly in front of the fire as the leather will harden and will be more likely to crack.

"*A good meal ought to begin with hunger.*"

French Proverb

LIDS

If you cannot unscrew a lid,
place the jar in boiling
water for a few minutes.
It should then become loose
and easy to unscrew.

LIGHT BULBS

You can delicately scent your
room by rubbing just a few
drops of your favourite perfume
onto a light bulb. A pleasant
smell will be emitted when the
light bulb is on.

LINEN

To prevent fine linen which
is not in constant use from
becoming discoloured and
yellow, wrap it in blue
tissue paper.

LINOLEUM

Unsightly black marks on linoleum floors can be removed quite simply by using a pencil-eraser. A few drops of paraffin in the water when washing will help make linoleum shine.

*"He who makes
no mistakes never
makes anything."*

English Proverb

LIPSTICK

When you are testing a lipstick
for colour, the best place to try
it is on the cushion of your
finger, where the skin is pinkish,
like the lips.

LOCKS

When you cannot get your key to turn in a lock, rub the key with vaseline, or, failing that, butter or margarine. This should help to ease the lock.

Alternatively, rub a key all over with the lead of a pencil and work it in the lock several times. This will help to keep the lock in good working order.

MATS

You can help to prevent the
edges of a mat from curling up
by pasting some very thick
starch along the edge and then
ironing over some brown paper
with a fairly hot iron.

MICROWAVE OVENS

You can help to remove stubborn and unpleasant cooking smells from inside a microwave oven by placing a teacup containing 3 parts water to 1 part lemon juice or vinegar inside it and cooking for eight to ten minutes on the lowest setting. Wipe the oven dry afterwards.

MIRRORS

If, before you run your bath,
you rub the bathroom mirror
with a few drops of shampoo,
this will help prevent it from
steaming up.

MOTHS

Small muslin bags filled
with aromatic plants placed
in your wardrobe and
drawers will deter moths
and will make your clothes
smell nice at the same time.

"Misfortunes always come in by a door that has been left open for them."

Czech Proverb

NAILS

When hammering small nails use a hairslide as a holder or stick plasticine over the area to hold the nail in position and protect your fingers.

To prevent cracking plaster when hammering in nails, first stick a piece of sellotape or masking tape to the wall, then hammer the nail in through the tape.

NAIL VARNISH

Storing the bottle in the fridge will prevent the nail varnish from getting a sticky consistency and it will help the varnish to last longer.

If the varnish thickens, it can be brought back to a better consistency by adding just a few drops of nail varnish remover.

OVENS

Next time you clean your oven,
after cleaning and drying it rub
it all over with a paste made of
bicarbonate of soda and water.
This should make it easier to
wipe clean next time around.

PAINT

When selecting a single colour for a room, choose one a shade lighter than you want, as paint tends to look darker once on the wall.

To keep the top of a paint tin clean, when painting place a paper plate over the top of the tin with the middle cut out. The drops will land on the plate which can be discarded afterwards.

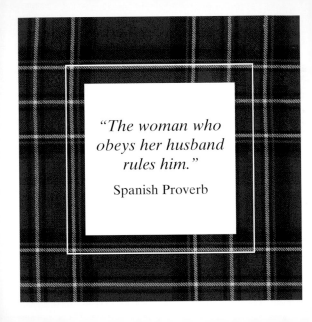

"The woman who obeys her husband rules him."

Spanish Proverb

PAINTBRUSHES

Dried out brushes can be restored to life by immersing them in hot vinegar, while errant bristles can be encouraged to return to their proper place by spraying the brush head with hairspray, smoothing and leaving to dry.

PAN

Before using a new pan,
boil some vinegar in it for a
few minutes to prevent food
from sticking.

PARCELS

When wrapping a parcel using string, first dip the string in warm water and then tie the knot. When the string dries it will shrink, leaving a tight knot.

PIANOS

Do not place a lot of books or ornaments on the top of a piano as it will deaden the tone.

If a piano key stays down when struck it is a sign of dampness.

Ivory keys will become yellowed more quickly if the lid of the piano is kept down, as ivory yellows more in the dark.

PINS

If you keep a small magnet in your pin box, then if you drop it the keys will be more likely to cluster around the magnet, making it easier to collect them.

PLASTERS

If you find removing sticking
plaster from your skin painful,
first rub baby oil over the
plaster. It should be easier
to remove.

"Since the house is on fire, let us warm ourselves."

Italian Proverb

REFRIGERATORS

A piece of charcoal placed inside your fridge will absorb the smells of strong food such as fish and cheese and will only need replacing every 5–6 months.

If your fridge is noisy it could simply be that it is not standing on a level surface.

RUBBER GLOVES

Avoid hands sweating in rubber gloves by dusting the inside of the gloves with talc when you use them and by washing the insides from time to time.
It will also help if you dry the gloves inside out after you have used them.

RUBBISH

To keep dogs and cats away
from your rubbish sprinkle pure
ammonia over the bags.

RUGS

To keep a rug from slipping or
wrinkling on a carpet or shiny
floor, stick some plastic stick-ons,
commonly used for the bath, on
the underside of the rug.

Alternatively, you could sew
or glue pieces of carpet,
pile downwards, under the
corners of the rug.

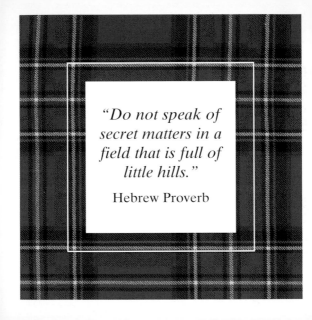

"Do not speak of secret matters in a field that is full of little hills."

Hebrew Proverb

RUST

Rust on utensils can be removed by rubbing the stains with a cork dipped in olive oil.

Rust stains on metal will sometimes disappear when rubbed with half a raw onion.

SCISSORS

To sharpen your scissors
cut a sheet of emery paper
into small pieces.

SHINE

Dark clothes can become shiny
with wear. Alleviated this by
brushing the shiny part with
black coffee – half a teacup of
strong black coffee to half a
teacup of water. Then press with
a cloth. Alternatively, rub with
a clean cloth dampened with
turpentine or white spirit.
The smell will soon disappear.

SHOES

When buying shoes, wait until the afternoon. Your feet are relaxed first thing in the morning but may swell during the day, so if you buy shoes early in the morning you may find they pinch in the evening.

When drying wet shoes, stuff with newspaper to help them keep their shape.

SHOWER CURTAINS

To prevent mildew on your cloth shower curtains, soak them for half an hour in a strong solution of salted water, then hang them up to dry.

Rubbing the curtains with bicarbonate of soda will also help remove mildew.

SLUGS

One of the less offensive ways
of killing slugs is by distributing
bran around the garden,
which they are attracted to
but which kills them.

Alternatively, you can entice the
slugs with a glass of beer left in
the garden overnight.

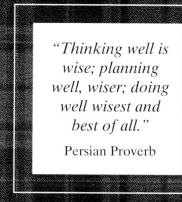

"Thinking well is wise; planning well, wiser; doing well wisest and best of all."

Persian Proverb

SMOKE

To prevent a room from becoming smoky when people are smoking in it, try lighting a few candles, or strategically arrange a few small containers filled with vinegar. This should help to eliminate the smoke from the room.

STAINS

When removing a stain, work
from the edge of the stain
inwards. This will help prevent
the stain from spreading.

STAMPS

To remove an unused stamp
from an envelope, submerge
that corner of the envelope in
boiling water for a few minutes.
The stamp should then come off
easily and can be left to dry.

Another method is to wet the
back of the stamp inside the
envelope with lighter fluid.

STICKY LABELS

Stubborn sticky labels on glass
or china can be removed with
nail-varnish remover, cooking
oil, turpentine or white spirit.

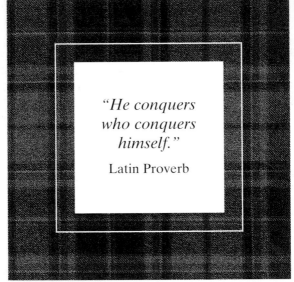

*"He conquers
who conquers
himself."*

Latin Proverb

THERMOS FLASKS

Stubborn smells and stains in flasks can be eliminated by pouring in a cup of boiling water and one tablespoon of raw rice. Shake for a few minutes then rinse.

If you will not be using your flask for a while, pop a couple of lumps of sugar into it to prevent mouldy smells developing.

THREAD

To prevent your double thread
tangling when sewing,
knot the ends separately
instead of together.

TOILET BOWLS

You can easily remove hard water marks inside the toilet bowl by pouring three teacups of vinegar into the bowl and allowing it to soak for a few hours before brushing and flushing.

WALLPAPER

When storing your rolls of wallpaper, keep them horizontal, not upright as the ends are more likely to get damaged if they are left standing up.

WASHING

To prevent dark clothes from picking up fluff when washing them with other items, turn them inside out before placing them in the washing machine.

WASHING-UP LIQUID BOTTLE

A clean washing-up liquid bottle filled with water is an ideal watering can for your house plants, enabling you to control the water and to avoid spillages.

"When spiders' webs unite, they can tie up a lion."

Ethiopian Proverb

WASTE-DISPOSAL UNIT

To clean your waste disposal
unit, sprinkle a dozen or so ice
cubes with some scouring
powder and pass them through
it, finishing with a few orange
or lemon peels.

WATCHES

If the glass of your watch gets misted up, turn it over and wear the glass next to your skin for a little while. The warmth from your skin will help to clear the mist.

WATERING PLANTS

If you are going away on holiday and can find no one to water your plants, keep them moist by soaking the soil thoroughly and then placing the plant and pot, still dripping, in a polythene bag. Close the bag tightly and place in a position where the plant will receive indirect sunlight.

WEIGHT

When you are keeping an eye on your weight, weigh yourself at the same time of the day once a week. This method will give you a truer idea of any weight loss or gain by counteracting any daily fluctuations.

"There is no home that is not twice as beautiful as the most beautiful city."

West African Proverb

WINDOWS

When painting window frames,
protect the glass from paint by
laying strips of dampened
newspaper along the edges and
in the corners. These will be
easy to remove afterwards.